Always THERE

A Children's Book About Healing from Grief

Written by:
Krystaelynne Sanders Diggs &
Nikki Woods Jones

Illustrated by:
Valeria Kornus

Copyright © 2023 Diggs Publishing

All Rights Reserved. No part of this publication may be reproduced, distributed, or transmitted in any form or by any means, including photocopying, recording, or other electronic or mechanical methods without the prior written permission of the publisher, except in the case of brief quotations embodied in critical reviews and certain other noncommercial uses permitted by copyright law.

ISBN: 978-1-961917-08-8

This book is dedicated to my Lola,
and every child that will experience
the death of a cherished loved one.

I miss you more than ever.
You are my guiding light.

Your spirit brings me comfort, each and every hard night.

Even though you are gone,
I still feel you near.

Love's an unbreakable bond that I'll always hold dear.

In all the moments I celebrate,
I know you'll always be there.
In every new memory I create,
Your presence there to share.

In nature I find peace.
Sunshine reminds me of you.

Together we release balloons, in loving memory of you.

Looking up at the moon,
are you looking at the sky too?

As the stars shine bright,
I wish you a goodnight.

Mornings come far too soon.
I enjoy watching our favorite cartoon.

It's okay to laugh and smile,
even if for a little while.

It's okay to be mad.
There are many reasons to feel sad.
I would give up anything,
Will you please come back?

They say grieving takes time.
Soon I'll be all right.
It's a mountain to climb,
but the future is bright.

I know in my heart,
you are with me forever.
We are never apart.
Never, ever, ever.

Your legacy lives in me.
Your spirit will never fade.

I know that you're free,
and I'm not afraid.

Life isn't fair.
But it also goes on.

You are always there,
here and beyond.

Letter:

We extend our heartfelt condolences for your loss.

This book was crafted to offer solace to your child and family during the grieving process. Our aim is to help you feel connected, reminding you that your loved one's presence is everlasting. Consider this book a conversation initiator, a guide, and a companion as you journey through grief.

By age eighteen, one in twelve children in the U.S. will face the loss of a parent or sibling (Judi's House, 2023). It's crucial to recognize that children process death differently than adults. Their reactions to the loss can profoundly impact their physical, emotional, and social well-being.

Natural Expressions of Grief:

Grief is deeply personal and non-linear. Its effects on a child's well-being can be long-lasting. Children may express their grief in various ways, including but not limited to: thumb-sucking, nightmares, separation anxiety, behavioral changes, bedwetting, sleep disturbances, irritability, assuming the role of the deceased, aggressive play, regression, academic struggles, profound sadness, depression, lack of focus, anger, withdrawal, appetite changes, suicidal ideation, and feelings of insecurity.

When to Seek Help:

Grief demands patience, love, and time. While assistance can be sought at any stage of grief, it's imperative to reach out immediately if your child struggles to cope, shows signs of severe depression, or exhibits intense grief reactions. Professionals like pediatricians, counselors, teachers, community centers, or religious institutions can offer invaluable support during this time, ensuring your child's well-being.

Ways to Support Your Child:

- Consult professionals like pediatricians, counselors, or teachers.
- Engage in open discussions about grief.
- Recognize and validate your child's emotions.
- Establish a comforting daily routine.
- Celebrate and memorialize the departed.
- Shower your child with extra love, care, and quality time.
- Assist your child in recognizing and articulating their feelings.
- Designate a special area for your child to mourn.

Grieving Tools and Resources:

Numerous tools and resources can aid in healing. Here are some methods we've found beneficial:

- Release biodegradable balloons during significant occasions in remembrance.
- Craft a blanket or bear using the deceased's clothing.
- Assemble a memory box adorned with photos and mementos.
- Plant a commemorative tree or garden.
- Dedicate a space for cherishing memories.
- Light a candle in their honor.
- Create a memorial space for remembering your loved one.

References:

Judi's House. (2022). Childhood bereavement estimation model. Retrieved from https://judishouse.org/research-tools/cbem/

American Academy of Child & Adolescent Psychiatry. (n.d.). Children and grief. Retrieved from https://www.aacap.org/AACAP/Families_and_Youth/Facts_for_Families/FFF-Guide/Children-And-Grief-008.aspx

Ehmke, R. (2023). Helping children cope with grief. Child Mind Institute. Retrieved from https://childmind.org/guide/helping-children-cope-with-grief/

The Child Mind Institute Family Resource Center. (n.d.). https://childmind.org/guide/helping-children-cope-with-grief/#block_184cfebc-d562-4aa9-bd6e-3534fec2020e

About the Authors:

Nikki Woods Jones is from Newport, Tennessee and currently residing in the Huntsville, Alabama area. Nikki is an Air Force veteran and currently works for the government. She became a widow in 2017. Nikki's husband passed away from Central Nervous System (CNS) Lymphoma at the age of forty-three. At the time, their daughter, Lola, was two years old. As a widow and mother, she wanted to co-write this book to provide comfort to other children and their parent/caregiver who are also grieving a loved one.

Grief share: Contact your child's school counselor and inquire about grief counseling services. Lola attends a grief share meeting once a month during her school day. Or you can request counseling services through the school.

Contact a grief support service in your area for your child to attend. The Caring House is a service provided through Huntsville Hospital in Alabama. Contact your local hospital to inquire about this service. The Caring House has provided grief support services for Lola. They have meetings for the children, one day grief summer camp with a butterfly release and memorial walk for the family, and support the child during the grief process.

Krystaelynne Sanders Diggs is a passionate children's book author dedicated to empowering young minds through literature. With a background in child advocacy and a deep commitment to creating safer and more informed communities, Krystaelynne has made it her mission to address essential topics that are often overlooked in children's literature.

Krystaelynne's advocacy work extends beyond her books. She actively collaborates with schools, organizations, and communities to conduct author readings, workshops, and seminars. Her goal is to equip children and their families with the knowledge and tools they need to navigate a complex world safely and confidently.

In addition to her books, Krystaelynne offers bulk discounts, school visits, and more. To learn more and stay updated, visit her website and follow her on social media.

Website: ksdiggs.com
Email: author@ksdiggs.com
Instagram: @allthingsdiggs
Facebook: Author K Sanders Diggs

Scan for Important Links:

Made in United States
Troutdale, OR
12/07/2024